From Start to Finish

MY LIFE AS A
HINDU

- Trevor Guy
- Sue Mizon
- Paul Morgan

DREF WEN

The Gayatri Mantra

Provider of life, Remover of pains and sorrows,
Giver of happiness, Creator of the universe.
Let us meditate on the brightness
of the Divine which destroys sin,
May it inspire and guide our minds
in the right direction.

Special Photography Pat and Charles Aithie (ffotograff)

Design Michael Leaman Design Partnership

The books in this series are also available in Welsh-language editions.

Photographs Liz Barry (ffotograff) front cover top left and foot right, pages 19, 22 top; Trevor Guy (ESIS) title page centre, pages 3 left and foot, 5 right, 6 upper centre and foot, 7 top and centre, 10 top, 11 centre, 13 foot, 14 all, 17 top and foot, 20 top, 22 centre, 26 top, 27 top and centre, 28 foot, 29; Nick Tapsell (ffotograff) front cover centre right, page 30 foot; Topham page 15; Nick Turner (ffotograff) page 11 foot. All other photographs are by Pat and Charles Aithie (ffotograff). Some of these (often indicated by corner mountings) are reproduced from photographs kindly provided by the families concerned. *Artwork* Pat Aithie pages 10, 30. *Map* Pat and Charles Aithie (ffotograff) page 6. We have made every effort to contact owners of copyright material and apologise if in any instance we have been unsuccessful.

Contents

Kanti: I have two sisters, Revti and Lakshmi. They are 15 and 10. My dad's a taxi driver in Cardiff but my mum doesn't go to work.

*Kanti: I have always lived in this area. It's very near to the **temple**.*

THINK ABOUT:

Why does Kanti wear the tilak mark?

What do you have in common with your friends?

Where do you like going with your family?

Are there different sorts of places you go with friends?

Kanti: I come along to the temple every day. The friends I see here are mostly the friends I have at school.

My community

KANTI My name is Kanti Halai. I like playing football and snooker. People would know that I'm a Hindu by the sign that I wear on my forehead. It shows that I belong to the Hindu community. It is a round dot, called a **tilak** mark. The two vertical lines show that we worship the **Vishnu** family of gods.

CHITRA My name is Chitra Prasad. I live with my family in Swansea and go to school here while my father is at university studying. My mother works in a nursing home. I have a sister called Chandni, aged 10, and a brother, Rajit, who is five. We also have my grandfather and grandmother living with us. We are one big family.

I was at the Ryan International School in Delhi, which is the capital city of India. We still have a flat in Delhi, and shall be going back there soon to live. My school here is a big school which most of the time I enjoy. Maths is much easier here than in India. In history I am doing European history but there it was Indian history. There are more children in a class in India, perhaps 35 or 40 in my class, but in some schools there may be 60 in a class.

Chitra: I don't go out with friends but with my family. We go to the park, the market or to somebody's house.

I have lots of friends in India and I've made new friends in Swansea. Our house is next to the rugby ground. It is OK living round here. Mostly people are very friendly but sometimes there is fighting and I don't like that.

THINGS TO DO

What sorts of things do people wear to show who they are or what is important to them? Draw some of these things and next to each picture write a sentence starting "If someone wears this, it shows that they…"

Chitra's family is very important to her. Her grandparents live with her family and older people are shown great respect in Hindu families. How would you like to be treated when you are old? You could write this as a letter to your grandchildren in the future.

Look through the book to find pictures which show what life is like in India. You could also look at books in your school library. Write a list of the things which Chitra would have found different from India when she came to Britain. You could do this as a chart:

Life in India	Life in Britain

Where my religion began

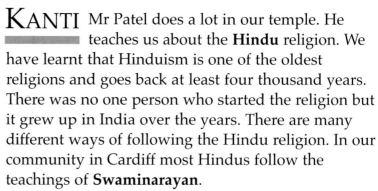

KANTI Mr Patel does a lot in our temple. He teaches us about the **Hindu** religion. We have learnt that Hinduism is one of the oldest religions and goes back at least four thousand years. There was no one person who started the religion but it grew up in India over the years. There are many different ways of following the Hindu religion. In our community in Cardiff most Hindus follow the teachings of **Swaminarayan**.

Swaminarayan went around all of India before settling in Gujarat in west India, where he preached. People started to follow his teachings. Following Swaminarayan is not a religion in itself but part of the Hindu religion. At the time of Swaminarayan there was nothing for the women, they were second-class citizens, but he changed that. He also built temples and set up schools. The main thing that he taught was that you had to live as part of the community for the good of everyone, not just yourself.

Our religion has had to change over the years. For example, some people will not eat anything unless it has been prepared in their own house. That is difficult when you are living in a country like Britain. The father and the mother might follow the rule closely but at school the children might try other foods which are nice to eat. Hinduism has survived because it has changed as time has passed, but the important beliefs still remain the same.

India

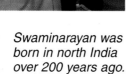

Kanti:
Mr Patel holds lessons in the temple on Saturday.

Swaminarayan was born in north India over 200 years ago.

THINK ABOUT:

Do all Hindus believe and do the same things? How do you know?

Swaminarayan believed that everyone should live as part of their community. How do people do that today in the area where you live?

What things have changed in your life as you have grown up?
Why do you think some things in Hinduism have changed over the years?

There are many huge, ancient temples in India.

6

Most people in India live in villages.

India is a mix of old and new, rich and poor.

THINGS TO DO

Find India on a globe or in an atlas. Name some of the countries which you would cross if you flew from India to Britain.

Most Hindus in India live in villages but there are also many great cities. Look at the pictures on this page and draw two different types of building, one found in a village and one in a city. What do you think it would be like living in each place?

Write a short story about a family in which the son or the daughter is tempted to do something which goes against what the parents believe is right.

Starting out in life

KANTI There are seven special times in life which we celebrate. Four are to do with the baby stage. The other three are **coming of age**, marriage and death.

After the baby is born the mother does not cook for 15 days and cannot come into the temple for 40 days. Then on the 40th day we have food, dancing and sing some songs to welcome the parents and baby to the temple. It is called a ras when we celebrate like this. The mother and father will worship together afterwards. At the end the **prasad** is given out, which the family of the baby will pay for.

A baby's name is usually chosen from the Hindu **scriptures**. Mr Patel, our teacher at the temple, told me that Kanti is another name for the sun god. Every name has got a meaning. Most names are religious names. When a child is born we look at a big chart, a **horoscope**, from which we select the initials. Once those are selected then the name can be chosen afterwards. If the horoscope says that the baby's name should begin with the letter K, then the name would be Kanti or Krishna, any name beginning with K.

Kanti: The parents name the baby at a ceremony at home.

Kanti: At the ras there is a dance which nearly everyone joins in, the men upstairs and the women downstairs. We go round in a large circle, doing the same steps all the time.

THINK ABOUT:

Have you been to a celebration of a baby's birth? What happened?

Why do you think the birth of a new baby usually makes people want to celebrate?

How do Hindu families celebrate the birth of a baby?

Kanti: The dance lasts for about 30 minutes and the music gets faster and faster until those that are left in are nearly running round. It's good fun but not many last to the end.

Chitra: This is me as a baby with my mother in our home in Delhi.

CHITRA When a baby is born he is blessed in the home on the sixth day. Later the baby's head is shaved, mostly before he or she is a year old. In Delhi my parents took me when I was very small to a temple near our house. In India you pay a barber to perform the shaving. The baby is then taken to the priest who performs the normal **puja**.

THINGS TO DO

Kanti is named after the Hindu sun god.
Draw a picture of the sun and round it write all the good things about the sun. You could make this into a mobile with the words hanging from your sun.

Make a list of all the children's first names in your class. Do a survey to find out how many think that their names can be found in a holy book. They might have to ask at home first. See if you can discover the meaning of some of their names.

Look at the pictures of the ras where the men and the women are dancing. Imagine you have been to the ras and write a letter to a friend to tell them about what happened. Describe the dancing, what you did and how you felt.

Kanti: Worship to thank God is part of welcoming the baby to the temple.

Following the path

Chitra: The holy books are treated with great respect.

CHITRA We don't have any one book which everyone believes you should follow. The oldest Hindu books are the **Vedas** and they were written in an ancient language called Sanskrit. It's mostly the priests who use those.

I don't use holy books to worship. I have read the **Ramayana** as a story book and watched it on television in India, so I know the stories. They help to teach us about the gods and what is right and wrong.

KANTI Swaminarayan looked through all the holy books and put them in a simple form. That book is now the Shikshapatri. "Shiksha" is knowledge, "patri" is booklet, so Shikshapatri means small book of knowledge. It gives rules for everyone – the rulers, the workers, the widows, anybody.

Chitra: In the Ramayana, the evil Ravana captures Sita, Rama's wife.

THINK ABOUT:

The Ramayana story tells how good overcomes evil. What other stories do you know which have the same message?

How does Kanti know what his religion does and does not allow him to do?

In Hinduism the gurus are thought to be wise people. Look at the picture of the guru. What do you notice about him? What do you think makes someone wise?

10

Kanti: I read the Shikshapatri every morning before I go to school.

CHITRA In India there are very important leaders called **gurus**. People travel from all over the world to visit them and ask for their advice and blessing.

I haven't been on **pilgrimage** but my grandparents have and my parents will be going. It requires a lot of planning. My father loves going to the hills, into the Himalayas. He wants to go to Badrinath in the beautiful Valley of Flowers. It is one of the four very holy places of pilgrimage in India and a good Hindu will go to all four to pray. My grandmother tells me Badrinath is a very exciting place and you will find lots of very important priests there.

Vijendra, a very important guru. Notice the sugar which he gives to his visitors as prasad and the red powder which he uses to put a red dot on their foreheads.

THINGS TO DO

Read or listen to the story of Rama and Sita. Draw one or more pictures or cartoons to show your favourite part of the story. Underneath write a few sentences to explain what is happening.

If you went on a special journey where would it be to and what would you do there? It could be a real place or somewhere in your imagination. Write a short piece to give the reader a good idea of your special place.

The Shikshapatri is Kanti's "small book of knowledge". Make your own little book of knowledge and in it write down the rules which you think would help you to lead a good life. You can decorate and colour the book if you wish.

A pilgrims' road into the Himalayas

Beliefs

Three gods in one – Brahma the creator, Vishnu who looks after the world, and Shiva who destroys things that are old and worn out, so that new life may be created.

CHITRA Belief in God is good. God blesses you and says, "Yes, you can do well in your life." That is what I believe. There seem to be many gods and it can be confusing.

KANTI I believe in God. We have different words for God. When I pray I use different names for God, but mostly I say, "Swaminarayan", who is the saint we worship as God. We also call Swaminarayan, "Lord". Our scriptures say we must believe in each and every god. We must believe in all gods. That includes gods of other religions.

It is not easy to talk about God. Mr Patel tries to explain God by saying that there is only the One God. Just as lots of different words, like strong, clever and kind, can be used to describe one person, so there are lots of different sides to God. Each side of God we give a name to, and look upon as a god or goddess. Lakshmi for example is the goddess of wealth, my sister was named after her. The gods can take human or animal form.

THINK ABOUT:

What is a lord? Why do several religions use "Lord" as a name for God?

What other names do you think would be good ways of describing God?

Hindus believe there is one God made up of many different parts. Mr Patel said that it is a bit like a person with one body but many different parts, like the head, hands, heart and so on. Can you think of other ways to describe this idea of one thing made up of many parts?

Chitra: One of my favourite gods is **Hanuman**, the monkey god, who helps Rama and Sita in their fight against the evil Ravana.

Krishna, an incarnation of the god Vishnu. He is very popular and there are many stories about him as a baby, a young man and a warrior.

THINGS TO DO

There are several pictures of Hindu gods in this book. Choose one of them to draw. Try to colour your picture carefully, using colours like the picture you have chosen. Write a label for it to name the god and say something about the picture.

Look at the pictures of the Hindu gods. Make a list of the ways in which the gods are different from human beings.

Write your own story about a time when the world was in great danger and it was rescued. You could use the idea of an incarnation of God in your story.

Sometimes when there is great evil or need in the world, God will come to earth. This is called an incarnation of God. When the job is done and the danger is past or the evil destroyed, the incarnation of God will leave. Krishna and Rama were incarnations. All incarnations are part of the One God. We believe that Swaminarayan is an incarnation of God.

There are two main families of gods. We follow the Vishnu family but there is also the Shiva family. **Ganesh**, the god with the elephant's head, belongs to Shiva's family and he is very popular as the bringer of good luck.

Ganesh, the god who helps to bring good fortune.

13

Right and wrong

Chitra: In this picture, the goddess Durga destroys an evil demon. Everyone will be punished at some time for what they do wrong.

KANTI I do wrong things sometimes. But if someone offers me a cigarette I say "No" because it damages your health. Taking anything which doesn't belong to you is stealing. The Hindu religion teaches that stealing is wrong. Vandalism and killing people are really bad. If one person kills another I think he should be locked up in prison for the rest of his life. We believe very strongly in not being violent. If I destroy someone, I am destroying a part of God. No-one has the right to destroy life. Only God has the right to do that.

SHIKSHAPATRI
My followers shall never kill, on purpose, any living creature, not even small insects.
(verse 11)

If I do something wrong, I have to try to put it right. I have to say sorry to God. I go up to the image of God and say that I am sorry.

CHITRA In India, if you do wrong, for example eat beef, you must first of all feel bad in yourself. Once you admit it the priest may not punish you, as long as he thinks you will not do it again. Or he may say that you have to come to the temple every day and chant God's name, say, a million times. Once you have finished that, you are clean again.

THINK ABOUT:

What does Kanti say are some of the things which he thinks are wrong? Do you agree with him? Why or why not?

How might a Hindu make up for things he or she has done wrong? How do you make up for what you have done wrong?

Would you stamp on a small insect that was in your path?

Chitra: In my school in India we made a poster about people talking to each other and learning to get on.

I do some things that are wrong, nothing serious. I always keep my bedroom very dirty and untidy. That's wrong. People should be very polite to everybody. They should talk nicely to older people and not use bad language.

I don't think it is right to kill. I think **Mahatma Gandhi** was right and people should never fight each other. We should not use violence. We should lead peaceful lives.

FACT FILE

Mahatma Gandhi An Indian leader who died in 1948. He taught that no-one should ever use violence to get his own way. Gandhi went on peaceful protests and was arrested and beaten many times, but never hit back.

Gandhi with his granddaughters, Mani and Ava, in 1947. Less than a year later he was shot, and died in Mani's arms.

THINGS TO DO

Look at the school notice board in the picture. What does it say about right and wrong? Make up your own school poster to say what you think is right and wrong.

Read the information sheet about Mahatma Gandhi. You could look for more information in your library. Prepare a short talk for the class or an assembly about the life of Mahatma Gandhi. You could record the talk on tape.

Chitra says, "We should lead peaceful lives." Write a poem to put across your idea of "a peaceful life".

Daily life

Kanti: *It's not hard praying every day. I was brought up to do it and I am used to it.*

KANTI Every day I pray in the morning and go to the temple in the evening. That way I am always reminded of God. Also, before we eat we have to say God's name as a sort of thanks.

There are other ways my religion affects my life. I don't eat meat, fish, eggs, onions and garlic. We don't eat meat because you can't have meat without killing animals. It's wrong to kill animals or anything at all. God has given life, so we shouldn't take it away.

The rules I follow are written down in our holy book, the Shikshapatri. I try to follow all the rules, but with some of them it's difficult. If I'm at school and want to eat some crisps I have to read the packet to make sure they contain nothing that's forbidden.

SHIKSHAPATRI
No-one is to eat meat, even in an emergency, nor drink wine.
(verse 15)

CHITRA For religious reasons, we don't eat beef. No-one in my family eats beef – it's bad! This comes from a belief in the cow as a **sacred** animal. The cow is like the **Mother Goddess** because they both give us so much. We are not **vegetarian** and I sometimes have school dinners. I just avoid beef and that's it. I like cheese and onion pizza best. I prefer that to Indian food, even in Delhi.

THINK ABOUT:

When you eat a meal, who has helped to make that meal possible? Do you thank anyone?

Why is it difficult sometimes for Kanti to follow his religion? Why does he try to keep to his religion in everything he does?

Why don't Hindus eat beef?

Food at Kanti's temple and in his home is always vegetarian.

Cows are allowed to wander freely in this street in Delhi.

Many Hindus in India start their day by making a pattern with rice flour on the ground outside their house. These patterns are called alpana. They are a form of worship and ask for God's blessing on the house for the day.

I wear mostly long skirts and dresses. I don't wear mini-skirts. I can choose what I want to wear. In India I would wear skirts and whatever I wear here. I don't wear a **sari**. Saris are normally worn after marriage or when you are grown up.

Alpana patterns outside a house in India

THINGS TO DO

Make up a menu of vegetarian food which Kanti's family could eat. You can draw and label the different items of food, cut them out and stick them to a paper plate for a display. You might like to include foods which are not grown in this country.

Make up a list of questions to ask the class about what they think it is right and wrong to eat. You could include questions about being vegetarian, eating only free-range eggs, eating sweets. Ask questions which can only be answered by a "Yes", "No", or "Don't know". If possible, use a database to show the results of your survey.

Draw a line down the middle of a page. On the left-hand side write down, in order, what you did yesterday. On the right-hand side, against each thing you did, write down a rule you had to follow to do it properly. For example –

Diary entry	Rule
7.00 a.m. Woke up and dressed.	I have to put on a clean shirt every day for school.

17

Growing up

Kanti: *Like my father, I have learnt the words of all the hymns we sing.*

KANTI I come to the temple on Sundays to learn about the Hindu religion. About twenty children of different ages come along. We take part in the worship too. Already myself and two of my friends lead the singing in the temple. That's quite a responsibility.

There is no fixed age for celebrating coming of age, when you become a man. When you think you are old enough, you can choose to have a celebration in the temple. This is usually held on your actual birthday, and anyone can come along. I have family who live in London and they come over to Cardiff for this sort of special occasion. We always have a good time when they come, with plenty of food. Becoming an adult is a religious occasion and the person performs an **arti** in the temple. This shows that you are making a commitment to being adult. I don't think it is too young to be thought of as an adult at 16 or 17.

CHITRA I used to ask my grandmother and mother about the gods because there was no school to teach me about religion. I was really very interested and they used to tell us stories when we were getting ready for bed. I shan't go through any ceremony which will say I am an adult now. When I get married it will mark the time when I shall be grown up.

For some Hindu boys there is a special ceremony, called the **sacred thread** ceremony. The boy will promise to learn the scriptures and obey his teacher. He will be given a circle of special cotton thread to wear. It goes over his left shoulder, across his chest and under his right arm. This reminds him of his duties. He will always wear a sacred thread after that.

THINK ABOUT:

How did Kanti and Chitra learn about their religion? Was it the same way?

What do you think are the main differences between being grown up and being a child?

How will Kanti celebrate his coming of age? How would you like to celebrate the time when you become an adult?

A group of boys wearing the sacred thread at a temple in India. These boys are now training to be priests.

THINGS TO DO

Think of a time when a number of members of your family came together. Was it to celebrate something? Write a short piece about what happened, why the family came together and how you felt at the time.

Draw a picture of someone wearing the sacred thread.
Briefly explain why it is worn.

At what ages do you think young people should be responsible? Copy and fill in the chart for yourself. You could then discuss each responsibility in pairs or small groups. Try to give reasons. Add other responsibilities if you can.

Responsibility	Age	Reason
Choosing own clothes		
Staying out with friends after dark		
Watching any television programme		
Getting married		

19

Worship in the home

Nearly all Hindu homes in India have a small shrine, however simple, where the family can worship.

KANTI Every morning I have a bath. That's part of my religious duty to be clean in mind and body. I am supposed to be up before sunrise but I don't always make it, especially in the summer. On a normal school day I get up at 6 o'clock. I worship every day at home so after the bath I start my puja. First I put the red dot and the two lines on my forehead. After that I set the gods out in the middle of the room and think about God. I stand on one foot, for about 20 seconds or sometimes longer. It helps me to concentrate. After that I walk round the gods about 80 times. Then I do the **darshan**, that's lying down in front of the gods. I put my hands together, then lie down on my front, like being asleep on the floor, then pray to God. Your mind should not be anywhere else but on the god whose picture is in front of you. It takes me half an hour to do my puja in the morning. It makes me feel good. It's like I am closer to God.

THINK ABOUT:

Why do you think Kanti stands as he does, on one foot, for some of his prayers? Think about how he holds his hands. (Look on page 16.)

What might people think about or talk about when they pray? Have you ever prayed? Do you think it is easier to pray if you are on your own or with other people?

How do the images help Kanti and Chitra to pray?

20

Chitra: *We just pray in front of the gods for about five minutes.*

Kanti: My mother cuts up food and offers it to God as part of her worship.

CHITRA Worship at home is very simple. We have **images** and photographs of the gods, they are of Ganesh, Rama, Krishna and others. We worship those gods because we have always worshipped them as a family. My mother will also place some **offerings** of food before the gods.

It is good to worship. It is what you should do. People worship God to be blessed by God. I believe you will do much better in your life if you worship God.

FACT FILE

Darshan Lying down in front of the image of a god shows that a Hindu knows he is in the presence of God. It is like someone bowing down in front of a king.

Image A picture or statue. A Hindu uses the word "murti" for the image of the god which he or she worships. The image or murti, like this one of Rama and his wife, Sita, helps a Hindu to think about God and what God is like.

Offering A gift, something that is offered to God in worship.

THINGS TO DO

Draw either Kanti or his mother worshipping at home. Write a sentence under your picture to say what is happening.

Make a drawing of one or two of the most special things you have in your house. Write a few sentences about them to say how you treat them and why they are important.

Kanti and Chitra worship at home because it makes them feel good and because they believe that it will help them do better in life. Write either a poem or a short story about "feeling good".

Worship in the temple

Chitra: Some temples in India are huge, with images of the gods on the tower.

CHITRA We go to the temple for puja about two or three times a month when we are in India. I like going. All the gods are there, like Shiva and Hanuman. There are small temples by our house but elsewhere there are also very big temples with towers made of marble. I go with my mother and sister and brother. We take some sweets and give them to the priest. He places them on the steps at the feet of the god. Then he closes the curtain in front of the god and after two or three minutes he opens the curtain and gives us back the sweets. They are then holy because the god has blessed them. The priest also makes a tilak mark on my forehead with red powder. It's a good feeling after puja, as though you can do everything you want to do.

KANTI Every evening about 100 men and women come along to the temple, but on Saturday and Sunday there will be more, perhaps 250. We come in and take our shoes off to show respect. First we praise God, then we put money in the plate or basket which is on the floor. After doing darshan we go to the picture of the god and pray to him and then walk round the **shrine**. We touch the big cushion on which the scriptures are kept, as a sign of respect for them.

Chitra: Some temples in the villages are very simple.

Kanti: To do darshan we lie down in front of the gods. Women pray separately in our temple.

THINK ABOUT:

Why might you give something good, like a sweet, to someone? What does that say about you as a person? Why do you think Chitra offers sweets to the gods?

What sorts of things do you do to relax? Why might Kanti find turning beads round relaxing?

How might you feel if you lay face down in front of someone? When Hindus do this in front of God what are they saying to God by their action?

22

To help us pray we take a **mara**. These are prayer beads and we keep them inside their bag all the time. I just keep turning them round. It helps me to relax.

I also take part in the arti. The **pujari** lights a candle in a lamp and offers the light to the gods while we sing the songs. God blesses the light and afterwards we all wash ourselves in the light from the flame as if it were water.

Kanti: *When using the prayer beads, many Hindus will just keep repeating a name for God, like "Krishna, Krishna, Krishna", over and over again.*

The arti ceremony

FACT FILE

Shrine The part of the temple where the images of the gods are kept. It is where the worshippers feel closest to God.

Mara In a mara there are 108 beads which represent all the main gods.

Pujari The person who leads the puja or act of worship. In most temples the pujari is a priest.

THINGS TO DO

Write down, or draw, or collect pictures of different ways that one person can show respect for another. Make a poster of them and give it a title.

Worship in a Hindu temple can be made up of lots of different activities. Read pages 22 and 23 again and look at the pictures. Note down all the forms of worship you can find. Can you add any more (look at pages 16, 17, 20 and 21)? Do any surprise you? Why?

Ask your teacher for a recipe for making Indian sweets. Make the sweets either at home or in class. Share them with others in your class.

Getting married

Kanti: *When Mum and Dad were married, Dad carried a sword. The sword shows that for the day you are a special person.*

KANTI My mum and dad had their marriage arranged for them by their parents. The two families knew each other when they lived in Kenya, before coming to Britain. Mum and Dad were allowed to meet first to see if they liked each other. My dad says that you don't have long to get to know each other, but once you're married you have to work things out. There has to be give and take. They could have said "No" to the marriage if they wanted. I expect my parents to choose a wife for me and I would be quite happy about that. It's how we are brought up. I think people should make promises to each other when they get married.

CHITRA I have been to my uncle's wedding so I know what happens. The couple go onto a stage and have **garlands** of flowers put round their necks. There is a fire which they walk round seven times and the priest says prayers and **blessings**. My uncle wore a suit and his bride wore a red sari. A bride's sari is nearly always red because red is meant to bring good fortune.

When a woman gets married she will usually go to live with her husband's family and will need to fit in with them. In Britain the couple will stay with the husband's parents for one or two years before going off to start their own home. In India they would stay with the parents for much longer.

Chitra: *The bride is blessed when the priest paints the top of her head with red paste.*

THINK ABOUT:

Why are most Hindus happy to let their parents choose the person they will marry?

Do you think that it is important for the families of the bride and groom to know each other well?

Which parts of a Hindu wedding do you find most interesting? Why?

Chitra: *At my parents' wedding they were given lots of beautiful garlands.*

KANTI When there's a Hindu wedding in Cardiff everyone in the community comes along. After the ceremony there is a feast. We all sit down to eat, then photographs are taken and the bride and groom are given presents. They get watches, jewellery, hi-fi stereo systems …

FACT FILE

Garland A ring of flowers placed round someone's neck to show they are very special and welcome.

Blessings Those things which make you happy and are seen to be a gift from God. A blessing can be words, actions, objects or simply feelings.

THINGS TO DO

Make a list of the promises which you think a man and a woman should make to each other when they get married.
Write it up neatly or use the computer to make it look like an important piece of paper.

Draw and colour an invitation card to a Hindu wedding. Use some of the information and pictures on these pages for ideas about colour and the sorts of things you might see at a Hindu wedding.

Imagine you are one of your parents. Write an advertisement for a wife or husband for you. It will need to describe you as you think you might be in at least 15 years' time.

WANTED HINDU
vegetarian bride for a Hindu bank worker, aged 36 years. Height 176 cms, salary 2,100 rupees per month. Reply with details Box 4112, Delhi.

BRIDEGROOM WANTED
for good-looking graduate girl. Respectable family, father Government Official. Reply with horoscope to Box XA2893, Madras.

SMART, INTELLIGENT
boy, in own computer business, with clean habits, seeks graduate girl, pretty, loving, co-operative and helpful at home and office. Reply Box 5623 Bombay.

Celebrating festivals

At Divali, sweets, such as barfi, are offered to the gods and eaten.

CHITRA There are hundreds of different festivals in India. **Divali** is my favourite because we have fireworks. At Divali we worship the gods Lakshmi and Ganesh. For the puja in our house there is a small plate which is filled with sweets and put in front of the god. Prayers are said from a holy book. After puja we go out and light the fireworks, sparklers and rockets. We also light **diva** lamps. It's nice when several are put on the window sills and you can see them glowing on your way home.

KANTI Everyone comes to the temple at Divali to pray and sing songs. It's different from our normal worship because we all greet each other and if we have been a nuisance to someone we say sorry. We greet each other by embracing. Of course men and women cannot touch so a woman will present a man with the gift of a coconut instead. Everyone will be wearing their best clothes and the children may be given presents.

Divali takes place in the autumn, usually in October. Divali is a bit like Christmas. Some Hindu families have celebrations at Christmas too, and at our temple we might have a ras on Christmas Day. In Mr Patel's home they have Christmas tea and presents for his children but he says it is expensive to celebrate Christmas and Divali!

THINK ABOUT:

Why do you think Chitra and Kanti both enjoy Divali best?

Why might Mr Patel's family also celebrate Christmas? Would you like to celebrate festivals from different religions?

Why do Hindus celebrate Raksha Bandhan? What is good about having a brother or sister?

HAPPY DIWALI

Kanti: It's good to send cards at festival time.

CHITRA At **Raksha Bandhan** my sister and I each tie a small bracelet round the wrist of our brother Rajit. The bracelet is called a **rakhi**. Rajit gives us some money or a small gift. I don't know the story behind the custom, but it is a way of showing affection between a brother and sister and of saying that we will look after each other. Rajit wears the rakhis just for the day because he is so young. Rakhis are not just for children. My father's cousins tie rakhis on my father's wrist and he wears them for several days. People go to the office wearing their rakhis. My grandfather who is 78 is still given one by his sister.

FACT FILE

Divali The festival of light celebrated in the autumn.

Diva A small clay lamp containing a candle or filled with oil. A wick made from twisted cotton wool is lit on Divali to show that light overcomes dark, just as the goodness of Rama overcame the wickedness of Ravana.

Raksha Bandhan The summer festival which recalls the story of when the god Indra was in danger. He was saved by his wife, who tied a special bracelet to his wrist to protect him.

Rakhi A cotton bracelet, often with a silver decoration.

THINGS TO DO

Draw a picture to show all the colour and fun involved in celebrating Divali.

Make your own rakhi. Use different colour threads to make it and tie on a small gift of some sort. Who will you give it to?

The Divali story is about good overcoming evil. Write an adventure story of your own where this happens. If you wish you can include characters with amazing, superhuman powers.

Working for others

Kanti: We are taught that it is good to give something each time we go to the temple.

KANTI At home I help with a few jobs, like doing some of the hoovering. I get asked to do that. My sister is asked to do more than me. I think girls know more about doing work in the house, and that boys have an easier time.

We collect money at the temple if there has been a disaster somewhere. If there was a flood in Bangladesh or famine in Africa, we would give to a charity like Oxfam. We also have a collection if someone is building a temple, or a school or hospital.

The adults give one-tenth of their wages to the temple and the temple will distribute to the needy. For example, we help students in India who are poor and cannot afford to go to colleges or buy the books they need.

CHITRA In India I have collected money and given to old people's homes. I have a gold medal and certificate from my school for that.

Once we went to a part of Delhi where some **Dalits** lived, to talk to the old people and the poor people there. We helped some of them to read. We gave them clothes and cleaned for them. It was very, very different from where I live. It was a good thing to do.

Chitra: We helped the Dalit women a lot and I'm glad I did it.

THINK ABOUT:

How do you help round the house? Why do you help? Or if you don't, why not?

How do Kanti and Chitra help others? Why do you think they do those things?

Have you ever given to charity or helped with a charity? Why did you do so and how did you feel about it?

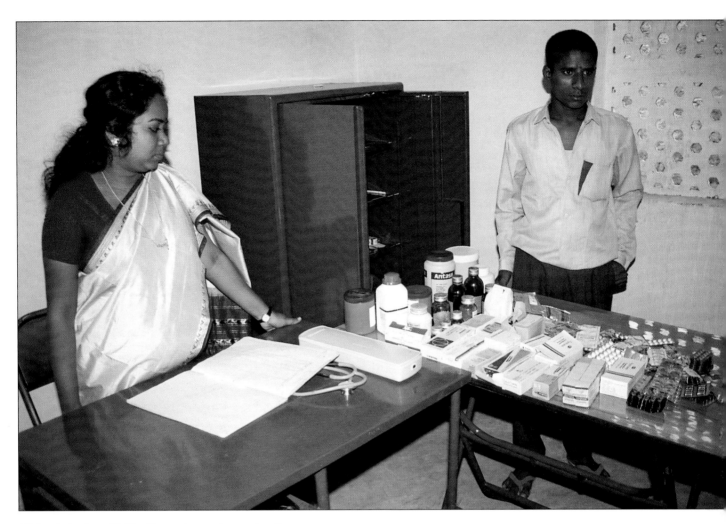

This clinic, in a Dalit village, is run by a charity.

At the temple we give money. It goes into a box. There aren't many charities in India which extend across the whole country, but there are many local charities which work to set up homes for old people and for children. There are some charities which work to protect cows.

THINGS TO DO

Design a poster asking people to help those who have been made homeless after a flood or earthquake.

Write a few sentences about the charity you would most like to help.

Imagine yourself as Chitra going into the poor part of Delhi to work with the people there. Write a page of your diary to say what you did and what you thought and felt about it.

FACT FILE

Dalits Hindus who used to be considered far less important than other people in Indian society. They had to do all the dirty jobs, like sweeping the roads. Today they have a better chance in life by being able to go to school, though many remain poor. In some places they still have to live apart from others. Gandhi tried to help them and called them "Children of God".

29

Dying

Kanti: We are born, grow up, grow old and die. Then our soul is born into another body and the cycle starts again.

KANTI When someone dies the body is burnt. We believe that the most important part of you, the soul, goes on to another life. It is born into another body. If you have been bad in your life, your soul might be born again into something worse, like a dog or a spider. If you have been good your soul will be born into a human being again, perhaps into a better life than the one before.

Mr Patel taught us that only people can tell the difference between right and wrong. Animals cannot. For dogs to eat meat or cows to eat grass, that is just what they do, they cannot help it. But humans can choose between good and bad.

Whoever comes back as a human being doesn't remember his past life. So when you become a human being, it is a chance for you to become wise and be good to people. If you then lead a very good life, your soul need never be born again into another body. Instead you can be with God forever.

There is no feast on the **cremation** day. After the cremation, prayers will be said at the person's home. Many people in the community will go to the house and listen to the prayers. Then on the twelfth day children are invited to the dead person's house to have a meal. After a month everybody in the community is invited for a meal.

In my house we have photographs of my dad's relatives who have died. It helps us to remember them.

THINK ABOUT:

Why do Hindus cremate (burn) their dead?

Why, while looking at the sunset, might Chitra say that there must be another life after this one?

Hindus believe that people can be reborn and come back as another person or an animal. What do you think?

Why do you think children are invited round for a meal to mark the end of the time of mourning?

The Burning Ghats on the banks of the ***River Ganges***, *where many families bring their dead to be cremated.*

CHITRA You don't expect a reward in this life or any other. All we should expect is to be at peace, to be strong and healthy. There are stories about people who say they remember their past lives. I don't know how true they are.

Chitra: There must be another life after this one.

THINGS TO DO

Draw your own cycle of life showing birth, life, death and rebirth. It could be about a person's life or about something else, like the seasons or the moon's passage.

When someone dies it is a very sad time. Write down all the ways people remember those they have known who have died, especially the good things about the person. Draw a picture alongside some of the ways you have noted.

Chitra believes that all we should expect from life is to be at peace, to be strong and healthy. Write a short poem or a paragraph to say what you expect from life.

FACT FILE

Cremation Burning a dead body. Hindus in Britain will do this at a crematorium but in India it is done out in the open. The eldest son has to light the fire on which the body is lying wrapped in a white cloth. If possible the ashes from the fire will be taken to the River Ganges and scattered on the water.

River Ganges The holy river in India which flows down from the Himalayan mountains into the sea. Hindus believe that anyone who bathes in it is blessed by God.

Index